polyam blues

Stephen Johnson

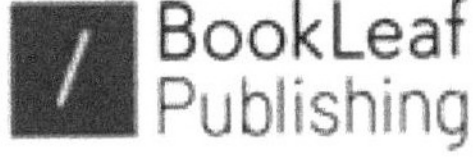

Presentation by *BookLeaf Publishing*

Web: www.bookleafpub.com

E-mail: info@bookleafpub.com

ISBN: 9789357211253

First edition 2022

DEDICATION

dedicated to the ones who used to be here

ACKNOWLEDGEMENT

thank you to the one who is still here

PREFACE

the following events are true
even the ones that aren't

brand new love

1

anyone
can become
someone

i don't fall in love i step into it

it's that same funny feeling the one
that no song could ever quite capture
the one that has you thinking about her
thinking about you does she and how
often the one that has you talking
for hours after everyone else has left
the one that has you talking to everyone
about her so much they probably want
you to shut up i'm so sorry i've talked
your ear off and i cannot put it back

it's that same old feeling the one
that feels new every time it happens
the one that makes you feel like everything
matters the one that makes you want
to be a better person the one where caring
for her is caring for yourself too the one
that makes you want to share yourself
with someone else the one that has you
pacing back and forth in your kitchen
wondering if it's worth the risk
to do this all again well of course it is

don't keep your hands to yourself

we're sitting in the brewery
our hands keep touching as we talk
but she doesn't move hers aside
i'm afraid to push it
but i don't think she would mind

we're strolling through the park
our hands keep bumping as we walk
getting closer every time
i'm afraid to push it
but i do it anyway she doesn't mind

we're standing at the front door
our hands are already together
fingers interlaced
moments away from our lips doing the same
i'm not afraid to push it
but she does it before i can
and i don't mind

a literal roach motel

she tells me she breeds cockroaches
for her bearded dragon
self-sustaining supply in a five-gallon tank
she says they're so expensive
that she started breeding them
instead of buying them
i tell her that's one of the most interesting things
anyone has ever told me
she thinks she's weird
i think she's cool

earl grey and early mornings

she makes tea for me
before i can make it myself
it makes me a little
uncomfortable
to have someone care for me
in this way
but i will never tell her
to stop

dining in

she's eating french fries
dipping them in cheese sauce
dressed in only
a fleece blanket

live fast dance slow

we're dancing under a pavilion
with one earbud in her ear
one in mine listening to the one song
i have saved to my flip phone
tranquil piano in one ear a thousand locusts
buzzing in the other a tiny snake slithers away
beneath our feet i like to think it knows
we would prefer to be alone

we're dancing at a bar downtown
with her friends and they don't know about us
but i think the music is too loud
and everyone is too drunk to realize
that we're hiding every touch
as the night ends her friend
asks me if i will get her home safe
not knowing that she's coming home with me

we're dancing in my living room
to a curated playlist in surround sound
swaying with her head nuzzled in my neck
my hands underneath her shirt one resting
on the small of her back one against the space
between her shoulder blades
she keeps saying it's getting late she should

probably head out in the next ten minutes
every ten minutes
and never makes her way to the door

the clock is my enemy

never enough time to say
everything i want to say
not enough words in the
english language to convey
the thoughts the feelings
the urges the longing
the desires the sensations
the sense of belonging
in every moment like they are
cut out of time just for us
cannot describe the connection
the attraction the depth of trust
the unfiltered honesty
honestly tell me anything
the smallest detail the broadest stroke
please tell me everything
about you

a different kind of dance

i push her red hair her brown hair
her blonde hair behind her left ear
i stare into her green eyes
her brown eyes her blue eyes
i taste her lips her tongue her teeth
i bite and she always bites back
i scratch her shoulder her back her chest
i lick her neck her stomach her breast
i give first but she always gives back
she likes it rough she likes it gentle
she likes it all
she's on top she's on bottom she's in a position
too difficult to describe
no matter what it always feels like the first time

things are going too well

it's that same funny feeling the one
that no poem could ever quite capture
the one that has you thinking about how her
demeanor changed how her smile doesn't
seem the same how her eyes look away
from yours more often than they did before
the one that has you asking if everything
is okay and she says it is but you hear
what she doesn't say louder than her words

it's that same old feeling the one
that feels worse every time it happens
the one that makes you feel like everything
is in shambles the one that makes you want
to be a different person in a different place
far away the one where caring for her
is eating away at you the one that gets you
pacing back and forth in your kitchen
wondering if it's still worth the risk
to do this all again well i guess it is

we need to talk

12

four innocuous
words arranged
in the worst
possible order

see you later goodbye forever

she leaves a letter goodbye
in my hand on the counter
inside the cover of a book
she writes in black ink in blue ink in pencil
she says i can't do this anymore
she says thank you for everything
she says i'm so sorry i love you goodbye
she says too little and too much
i could read this a thousand times
and it would never be enough

...

14

someone
can become
someone you used to know

what they leave when they leave

she leaves the scent of her
perfume on a blanket i refuse
to wash until the smell fades
she leaves plans written
on the calendar weeks in advance
that were never officially canceled
she leaves an empty hanger
where my favorite shirt used to be
she leaves my house keys among
a pile of loose change and earrings
she leaves episodes of our favorite
show unwatched movies never
to be watched again
she leaves a tissue with black
lipstick smeared in it a coffee mug
with pink lipstick on the edge a shot
glass stained with the residue of vodka
she leaves her watch that beeps
every hour on the hour reminding
me how long a day can be
she leaves an afterimage of her
smiling at the front door
she leaves breath exhaled
a laugh echoing in the halls
words hanging in the air

in bloom

flowers bought in a different time
the giver is gone
yet they still remain
dinner table cluttered with petals
never thrown away
how envious i am
of how easily they
shed their skin
and discard their limbs

my virtues are everyone else's vices

medical experts estimate
it takes about two weeks
for the average laceration to heal
what about wounds
too deep for any sharp instrument
to reach the bottom of

good. you?

how are you
i'm fine thanks for having
nice weather we're asking
how are you
i'm alive still alive living the life
staying alive johnny five alive living the dream
how are you
it's fine i'm fine everything is fine
fine wine fine point fine line finely shredded
how are you
oh i'm good it's knives to see you
well i know you're busy
i won't keep you sever you later
all worries you're good no problem
we'll cut up with each other soon

pity party of one, i

what did i learn what does it matter
what did i gain but a massive relapse
from a major lapse in judgment
a momentary lapse of reason
there is no lesson there is no meaning
we're just stupid scared horny meatbags
wandering aimlessly
bumping into each other
in one big dark room on this
floating spinning rock
messy creatures making messes
looking for someone to help clean them up
waiting to love and be loved
to hurt and be hurt

pity party of one, ii

i want the love i want the hurt
i want to make a mess and step into another
i want to make several at the same time
and i never want to clean them up
just leave it there make it worse i don't
want to fix you in fact i don't think
there's anything to repair but if you
think you're broken then please stay
broken here with me i'll be your human
sink drain all your sins and fears and pain
into me i'll be your own personal
emotional sponge bleed into me
and wring me out as needed
i'll be your favorite homewrecker
distraction escape you'll never have to leave
i don't care if you have to lie to everyone else
but you'll never have to lie to me

pity party of one, iii

she says i should hate her for this
but she's done no wrong so there is
nothing for me to forgive sure
this would be easier with someone
to blame so i guess i'll blame myself
please blame me too after all
it's my fault for getting so involved
with someone so involved with...
but i'm not afraid of the mistakes
we've made i'm not afraid of the harm
we cause each other and ourselves
i don't shy away from the awkward
i don't hide away from the painful
this is what it means to be alive
do what you what to do with your
time do it with conviction commitment
completely with every fiber of your
being no one is rational no one is logical
we are perfectly imperfect
i need no apologies you owe me nothing
you'll never have to explain yourself
to me but you can if you want to
i hold no grudges i will love you
regardless i'll leave you with a promise:
i will always be here for you
just as i have always been here for you

it's okay and if it's not it will be

i'll make the same
mistakes again
but next time
i'll make them better

www.ingramcontent.com/pod-product-compliance
Lightning Source LLC
La Vergne TN
LVHW051249200726
843510LV00011B/1759